# FREE AT LAST from Oppression

Jerry Savelle

# FREE AT LAST FROM OPPRESSION

ISBN 0-9702911-1-6

Unless otherwise stated, all Scripture quotations are taken from The King James Version of the Bible.

**Supplier**

**JSMI(UK)**

**PO Box 193**

**Newport, South Wales**

**NP20 1XN UK**

**Tel: +44(0) 1633 256363**

# Contents

# Chapter 1

# 1

## "Lord, I'm in Over My Head!"

You storm out of the house, get in your car, lock the doors and prepare to just drive away. Where? It doesn't matter. Just away from everything! You can't take it anymore. You're miserable. You're frustrated. You're tired of trying to make things work that simply aren't working. Instead, in your extreme frustration, you lay your head against the steering wheel and just cry out to God, "Lord, please help me. I'm in over my head." You don't know where to go, what to do or how to change the circumstances around you. Torment, confusion, hopelessness, misery, pain — ***oppression*** is what you're under.

***Oppression*** is defined as *the act of oppressing, the imposition of unreasonable burdens; the state of being oppressed or overburdened; misery; hardship, grief, calamity, depression, dullness of spirits; a sense of heaviness.*

***Freedom*** is defined as *the state of being exempt from the control of another.*

I've written this book for the sole purpose of telling you this: Jesus is the Oppression-Lifter! He came to set you free from the control of oppression. You don't have to live your life as it is right now. You don't have to lay in bed crying, worrying and afraid another night. You don't have to go another day just surviving your circumstances. You don't have to accept that things will never change in your situation. Jesus is the Way-Maker. He makes a way where there seems to be no way - to bring you peace, hope, joy and love in the midst of impossible, heartbreaking situations.

You're not alone. No matter what the devil may tell you, you are not alone. God intends to see you set free spirit, soul and body. So, wipe your tears, pull your shoulders back, hold your head up and let's get on the road to your recovery.

**Save me, O God; for the waters are come in unto my soul. I sink in deep mire, where there is no standing: I am come into deep waters, where the floods overflow me.** ***I am weary of my crying: My throat is dried: mine eyes fail while I wait for my God.***

– Psalm 69:1-3

Can you relate to what the Psalmist was feeling? Are you tired of all the crying? Do you feel like you've cried all the tears you could possibly shed? Are you just waiting on God to *do something?*

**But as for me, my prayer is unto thee, O Lord, in an acceptable time: O God, in the multitude of thy mercy hear me, in the truth of thy salvation. Deliver me out of the mire, and let me not sink: let me be delivered from them that hate me, and out of the deep waters. Let not the waterflood overflow me, neither let the deep swallow me up, and let not the pit shut her mouth upon me. Hear me, O Lord; for thy lovingkindness is good: turn unto me according to the multitude of thy tender mercies.** ***And hide not thy face from thy servant; for I am in trouble: hear me speedily.***

– Psalm 69:13-17

The Message translation reads this way, **. . . God save me. I am in over my head** (Psalm 69:1). In other words, the Psalmist is saying, "I am in trouble, and I need some quick results." Does that describe how you feel right now? Do you need a miracle in your life? Do you need a breakthrough? Do you need God to change some things in your circumstances?

That phrase, "I'm in over my head" just really stood out in my spirit. When the Lord gave me this message, I could see people in their homes and in their cars on their way to work saying, "I am in over my head. Lord, I don't know what to do. Please help me."

Your situation may look hopeless, but it is not hopeless. We serve the God of hope. The God we serve can turn it around. He is a master at turning adversity into victory.

The Message translation in Psalm 69 reads: **God, God, save me! I'm in over my head . . . Don't let me go under for good. . . . Now answer me, God, because you love me; Let me see your great mercy full-face . . . Come close, God; get me out of here. Rescue me from this deathtrap.**

I've had times when I've said, "Dear God, I am in over my head. What in the world am I doing out here? How did I ever get into this mess?" Most of the time, when people cry out for mercy, it is because they have gotten themselves in a mess.

When you ask for the mercy of God, you are saying, "God, please overlook my mistakes, my bad decisions. Please overlook the mess I've gotten myself into." Crying for mercy is a sign of desperation. When you get in over your head financially and your outgo is greater than your income, then your upkeep becomes your downfall. Then, you begin wondering where in the world the money is going to come from. You ask, "How did I get into this mess?" And the Holy Spirit gently says, "You did it by over spending, impulsive buying, and bad management."

Don't put the book down now. I plan to help. I'm going to give you the answers that will set you on the path of freedom. I want to help you open your eyes to the truth and then the truth will set you free.

## Need Quick Results?

Not knowing what to do or how to change your present condition can be one of the most miserable, lonely feelings in the world. When you feel as though you're in over your head, Satan can make you feel absolutely hopeless. He will attempt to magnify your problems so that you can't see the solution. There **is** a solution to what you're going through. Did you read that? There is a solution.

The spirit of hopelessness can come on you when you least expect it. You can be in a service where the praise is high, and you are rejoicing and then you can walk out of the building, get in your car, and that feeling of despair almost consume you. You think, *"God, what am I going to do?"*

Those feelings and negative thoughts will wake you up in the middle of the night. You could be sound asleep and suddenly, you break out in a sweat and your head is screaming at you, *"What are you going to do? You are in over your head. How in the world are you ever going to get out of this mess? There's no hope. It will never change. You blew it. You're finished."*

Those are all lies from Satan to keep you frightened, depressed, wondering and worrying about what to do. It's all an attempt to get you to run ***from*** God rather than run ***to*** God in the middle of your storm. I can understand the Psalmist when he was crying out, "God, I am in trouble. I don't know what to do, but I am calling on You. I believe You will answer me because You love me. I am asking for Your mercy. And if at all possible, please do it quickly" (Author's paraphrase).

Your problems may look so impossible that it seems as though not even God can get you out of this situation. Peter felt that way. In the book of Mark, Peter and the disciples were out on the sea and a storm came up. Jesus was asleep in the back of the ship, and Peter woke Him up saying, "You don't even care, do you? We are about to drown and what are you doing? Sleeping! You don't even care" (Author's paraphrase).

I'm sure you've thought that God didn't care about the storms you were experiencing at times. You may not have said it like Peter did, but you thought it. There is nothing more discouraging than feeling like it is all over, you're finished, nothing can be done, and you're all alone. When your head sinks down into your hands, the worry begins and the devil starts screaming, "There is no hope. There is no way. You might as well throw in the towel." He will also tell you that nobody around you cares about what you're going through and not only that – God doesn't even care! "You are in this alone. You might as well give up and die."

## Satan Is A Liar

**. . . When he speaks a lie, he speaks from his own resources, for he is a liar and the father of it.**

– John 8:44
The New King James Version

As I wrote earlier, I want you to grasp the truth that Satan is a liar. What you've been hearing is a lie. He is the father of all lies. He cannot speak the truth. It's impossible for him. It's also equally impossible for God to lie. He is the God who cannot lie. So, wouldn't it be wise to read what God says and declare that over your life?

**Fear not, for I am with you; Be not dismayed, for I am your God. I will strengthen**

**you, Yes, I will help you, I will uphold you with My righteous right hand.**

– Isaiah 41:10
The New King James Version

If you really paid attention to that scripture, then that alone should assure you that everything is going to be alright. You are not alone. You have Almighty God on your side, and He will not let you be destroyed. He **will** help you. He will **help** you. He will help **you!**

You may not have any physical evidence, in the natural, that would indicate to you that you are coming out of this hard time. Just the fact that God loves you, and He says in His Word that He is with you, may be all that you've got to hold on to. Well, hold on to that! You do have something to hold on to. And it's a pretty awesome promise from the Creator of this Universe. He is not going to just sit back and allow you to be destroyed.

### God Loves You, Regardless

Sometimes you might feel as though you don't deserve His unconditional love, but He loves you anyway. Even when you make mistakes, He loves you. Even when you got yourself into trouble, He loves you. Aren't you glad that His love never changes?

### "Lord, Have Mercy On Me"

Remember the Psalmist said, "Let me see your mercy." When someone cries out for mercy, it indicates that there is nothing they can do in themselves to change their circumstances. It is recognizing that you don't have the wisdom to handle this situation. You don't have the power, the means, the resources, the strength or the ability to change your circumstances so you are dependent on God. You ***have*** to trust God in this situation. If you are to be delivered, then you know it is going to be because God's mercy was manifested.

There was a man in the tenth chapter of Mark named Bartimaeus who was blind, and a beggar. He heard that Jesus had come to his village. Even though Bartimaeus couldn't see Jesus, he heard the crowds. He heard them talking about this man, Jesus. Bartimaeus had heard about the miracles of Jesus and it stirred his faith. He finally thought there could be hope for his life. And there Jesus was, standing on his street where he sat and had begged for years. When Jesus arrived, he began to cry out, "Thou son of David, have *mercy* on me."

When he cried out for mercy, he was saying, "I am powerless to change my own circumstances. There is nothing I can do, but I am dependent on You. I am asking for Your mercy." When he cried out for the mercy of God, the people told him to be quiet. The Bible says, "He cried the louder" (Mark 10:48). He was desperate for a miracle. He wanted results. He didn't care what anybody else thought about it. He did not care what anybody else said. He was determined that if anybody was going to get a miracle, it was going to be him because the Miracle Worker had come to town.

When Jesus confronted him, He said, "What do you want Me to do?" He said, "I want you to recover my sight. I want you to deliver me from this blindness" (Author's paraphrase). Notice, he associated *mercy* with *healing.* He associated mercy with the miraculous. He cried out for mercy. He didn't say, "Jesus, heal me."

He said, "Jesus, thou Son of David, have mercy on me." In his mind, mercy produced miracles. Mercy was synonymous with healing, deliverance and miracles. So, Jesus gave him his miracle. He opened his eyes and he could see.

The W. E. Vines Dictionary describes ***mercy*** as *the outward manifestation of God's compassion.* It is the benevolence of God towards those who are hurting. The mercy of God implies *tenderness* or *kindness.* It is also *an act of favor.* When you ask God for mercy, you are asking God for a favor. You are saying that you are powerless to change your circumstances; therefore, you need the mercy of God.

In Ephesians 2:4, the Apostle Paul wrote, **But God, who is *rich in mercy* . . .** That would simply mean that God has no shortage of mercy. He can give you as many favors as you need. Just how big of a favor do you need? The Message translation says - **Immense in mercy and with an incredible love . . .**

It makes no difference how impossible your situation looks or how big your need might be; the mercy of God, in manifestation, brings with it adequate resources to meet any need. You need to cry out for the mercy of God right now. He hears your cries, and He will answer.

### God Will Comfort You

**. . . the Father of mercies, and the God of all comfort; Who comforteth us in all of our tribulation . . .**

– 2 Corinthians 1:3-4

Our Heavenly Father is known as "the Father of mercies" and "the God of all comfort." When you feel like you are in over your head, He is the God of all comfort. The Message translation says - **He comes alongside us when we go through hard times, . . . rescued us from certain doom.** He is right there with you helping you through these hard times that you are experiencing.

Satan may be telling you that there is no way out. The Message translation calls that "certain doom." If you are being told that the sickness in your body is incurable, the Message translation refers to that as "certain doom." If you were told, "Sorry, we are going to have to repossess," the Message translation refers to that as "certain doom." The Word of God says He is the Father of mercy; the God of all comfort and He rescues His own out of certain doom. It is not over as long as the mercy of God is available to you and me.

**Gracious is the Lord, and righteous; yea, our *God is merciful.* . . . I was brought low, and *he helped me.* . . . thy rest, O my soul; for the Lord hath dealt bountifully with thee.**

– Psalm 116:5-7

**. . . when I was at the end of my rope, *he saved me.* I said to myself, "Relax and rest. *God has showered you with blessings . . .*"**

– The Message Bible

You may be at the bottom today. You may be at the end of your rope. You may be spending many sleepless nights not knowing what else could possibly be done to turn your situation around. You may have been given this book by a friend or you bought it as a last resort searching for hope. I want to encourage you today: don't give up. Don't quit. It is not over. Just because the circumstances indicate that it is and just because the devil is saying that it is, it is not over. As long as there is mercy, as long as you serve the God who is gracious and full of compassion, it is not over. Your best days are just ahead. Your future is still bright. It doesn't matter what you've done or how bad you think you've messed up, God will turn this entire situation around for His glory and you will be smiling, rejoicing and you will be free again!

You may be in over your head right now, but I want to paint a picture of where you are headed – "showered with blessings." That is the mercy of God. That is the favor of God. That is the compassion of God. That's the reason the devil is screaming at you like he is. He does not want you to experience these showers of blessings. Obviously, if you give up, there will be no manifestation of the shower of blessings. If you call it quits, if you turn your back on God, if you quit going to church, if you quit reading faith-building material, if you get discouraged and say, "I don't want any part of this. It doesn't work," you just did exactly what the devil hoped you would do.

Look at what you would miss out on as a result of it . . . showers of blessings. That ought to motivate you to keep on standing, keep on reading, keep on confessing, keep on praying, keep on believing for a breakthrough! That is why it is so important that you refuse to give up even when you feel like you cannot take anymore. Showers of blessings are coming your way. You will experience freedom from this oppression. The mercy of God is headed your way!

# CONFESSION

*He shall call upon me, and I will answer him:*
*I will be with him in trouble;*
*I will deliver him, and honour him.*
*With long life I will satisfy him,*
*and show him my salvation.*

– Psalm 91:15-16

*In my anguish I cried to the Lord, and he*
*answered by setting me free.*

– Psalm 118:5 (NIV)

*He that trusteth in his own heart is a fool:*
*but whoso walketh wisely,*
*he shall be delivered.*

– Proverbs 28:26

*But we had the sentence of death in ourselves,*
*that we should not trust in ourselves, but in*
*God which raiseth the dead: Who delivered us*
*from so great a death, and doth deliver:*
*in whom we trust that he will yet deliver us.*

– 2 Corinthians 1:9-10

# Chapter 2

# 2

## "God, Do You Remember Me?"

If you're experiencing oppression, you're probably just trying to keep your head above water. You may be doing everything you know to do just to survive. It may seem that every time you turn around, there is another attack facing you. You may have begun to wonder if God even hears your prayers at all. "Why isn't anything changing if God really hears me?" I want to encourage you today that God does hear your prayers. He hears your cries. He sees your pain. He wants to heal your broken heart and restore your soul, but you have to ***trust Him*** to do it.

Even though it may look like nothing is happening, God is working behind the scenes. He ***is*** working on your behalf.

**For it is God which worketh in you both to will and to do of his good pleasure.**

– Philippians 2:13

If you are willing to trust Him and put your life in His capable hands, not trying to make things happen yourself, then God will provide a way to help you overcome every obstacle in your life. He knows what He is doing.

**Wherefore let them that suffer according to the will of God commit the keeping of their souls to him in well doing, as unto a faithful Creator.**

– 1 Peter 4:19

**So if you find life difficult because you're doing what God said, take it in stride. Trust him. He knows what he's doing, and he'll keep on doing it.**

– The Message Bible

When you decide you are going to believe the Word of God, that does not mean you get a free ride through earth for the rest of your life. In fact, doers of the Word come under greater attack than anyone else because they are the most dangerous to Satan. When you decide that you are going to do the Word, and you are going to believe God, Satan comes immediately to steal your focus.

Did you notice that when you started tithing ten percent of your finances to God, your finances came under attack? Satan will attack your finances hoping that if he creates enough pressure for you financially, then you will quit tithing. Don't fall for it. The pressure can't last forever. It's just a smokescreen. He knows your finances will greatly increase as a result of tithing so he's trying to keep you from being a faithful tither.

God knows what He is doing. Sometimes we don't know what God is up to, but He knows what He is doing. The greatest revelation you will ever receive in your life is that God is smarter than you. Sometimes it doesn't look like God is doing a thing. Sometimes you may even feel like asking, "God, do you even know that I am still here? Have you forgotten my name? Should I send you a postcard with my address?" God is well aware of what you are going through. He is well aware of what you need.

The Bible says in Matthew 6, that He knows your needs even before you ask Him. And it is His will to fulfill every need in your life (Author's paraphrase).

## Don't Quit Now

If life seems to be getting more and more difficult because you are doing what God says, take it in stride. Trust Him. God has a plan. We can rest assured that while we are trusting Him, He is busy rearranging things. He is always a step ahead of us. Our job is to simply trust Him.

Many times we try to figure out how things are going to work out. We try to do it ourselves. We try to make things happen. When we do that, we are saying, "God, I don't think you're capable of handling my situation, so I'm going to do it myself."

When you put your situation, your circumstances, your trouble in God's hands, He will work it out. And usually, it will be in a way that you could never have dreamed up.

Let's look at the story of Elijah.

**And the word of the Lord came unto him, saying, get thee hence, and turn thee eastward, and hide thyself by the brook Cherith, that is before Jordan. And it shall be, that thou shalt drink of the brook; *and I have commanded the ravens to feed thee* there. So**

**he went and did according unto the word of the Lord: for he went and dwelt by the brook Cherith, that is before Jordan.**

– 1 Kings 17:2-5

Notice God was already ahead of the situation. He was already ahead of the circumstances. He didn't say, "You get moving and I will try to figure out something to do." Isn't it interesting that He chose ravens (birds) and not people to meet the prophet's needs? Sometimes people are hardheaded. Sometimes people won't obey.

Some would say, *"Surely God doesn't want me to feed that guy. I don't even know him."* But birds don't argue with God. They didn't say, "We are not doing it. Let the cows do it. We did it last week." They did exactly what God told them to do and notice the prophet was sustained.

**And it came to pass after a while, that the brook dried up, because there had been no rain in the land. And the word of the Lord came unto him, saying . . .**

– 1 Kings 17:7-8

Notice how important it is to get into position to hear the Word of the Lord. When you are trusting God, He will tell you what to do. You just need to be sensitive to His voice.

**Arise, get thee to Zarephath, which belongeth to Zidon, and dwell there: behold, I have commanded a widow woman there to sustain thee.**

– 1 Kings 17:9

Isn't it amazing that when the prophet had no idea where or how he would eat, God was always arranging things for him as long as he obeyed His voice. When you have no idea how your life can turn around or how you can get out of the situation you've found yourself in, God is arranging your way of escape. Your job is to listen to Him and obey His voice. Don't try to figure it out on your own.

## God is Working Behind the Scenes

I seriously doubt that the prophet could have dreamed up the birds feeding him. Only God could have arranged that. You can't dream up how God can meet your needs or answer your prayers, so don't. Just let God arrange the details. Give Him your faith and watch what He will do.

**So he arose and went to Zarephath. And when he came to the gate of the city, behold, the widow woman was there gathering of sticks: and he called to her, and said, fetch me, I pray thee, a little water in a vessel, that I may drink. And as she was going to fetch it, he called to her, and said, bring me, I pray thee, a morsel of bread in thine hand.**

**And she said, as the Lord thy God liveth, I have not a cake, but an handful of meal in a barrel, and a little oil in a cruse: and, behold, I am gathering two sticks, that I may go in and dress it for me and my son, that we may eat it, and die.**

– 1 Kings 17:10-12

Notice the birds obeyed, but the woman gave an excuse as to why she couldn't do what God told her to do. The first thing you and I might have thought was, *"Boy, did I miss God. God told me to go to this widow woman's house and she doesn't have enough to feed her and her boy . . . much less, feed me. She is talking about dying after she has lunch. Did I ever miss God!"*

But he believed he heard from God.

**And Elijah said unto her, Fear not; go and do as thou hast said: but make me thereof a little cake first, and bring it unto me, and after make for thee and thy son.**

– 1 Kings 17:13

He believed that if she would do what God instructed her to do, somehow, someway, God would make provision for her.

**For thus saith the Lord God of Israel, the barrel of meal shall not waste, neither shall the cruse of oil fail, until the day that the Lord sendeth rain upon the earth. And she went and did according to the saying of Elijah: and she, and he, and her house, did eat many days. And the barrel of meal wasted not, neither did the cruse of oil fail, according to the word of the Lord, which he spake by Elijah.**

– 1 Kings 17:14-16

In this story, we can see how God was working behind the scenes not only for the prophet, but for this little widow woman as well. She had a need in her life, and God not only made provision for the prophet, but He made provision for the little widow woman as well. That should answer any questions you may have had about God only providing for preachers. God proves once again that He is no respecter of persons (Acts 10:34).

**. . . It makes no difference who you are or where you're from.**

– Acts 10:34
The Message Bible

All God is looking for is trust. God is looking for faith. Can you believe Him? Can you trust Him? Do you really believe that God loves you so much that He would come to your rescue if you called on Him in faith?

How many times do you suppose you missed out on something God was arranging because you quit trusting Him right at the last moment? I don't know about you, but that motivates me. That motivates me to keep believing God, keep standing, keep praying, keep confessing the Word, keep doing everything I know to do. Don't get weary in well doing because you never know when you are about to experience a due season. Praise God.

Your due season could happen in church. Your due season could happen after you leave church. Your due season could happen at anytime, any place as long as you are trusting God.

### God Cares About The Details

**That's why we can be so sure that every detail in our lives of love for God is worked into something good.**

– Romans 8:28
The Message Bible

When people say that your situation is just too impossible, then that is when God will come through and prove to you that He is the God who specializes in doing the impossible. A ***miracle*** has been defined as a *work wrought by divine power by means beyond the reach of man.*

In other words, you can't do it. You can't make it happen, but that is when God steps in. God is still the Miracle-Worker today. Miracles show us that God is not only **able** to meet our needs, but **willing** to meet our needs. Miracles are acts of God's favor toward those He loves.

Splitting the Red Sea was an act of God's love (Exodus 13 & 14). Getting water out of a rock was an act of God's love (Exodus 17). Giving manna from heaven was an act of God's love (Exodus 16). Multiplying the widow's cruse of oil and enabling her to pay off her debt was an act of God's love and favor (2 Kings 4). If He will do it for those people in the Old Testament, then how much more will He do it for New Testament people? We have a better covenant founded upon better promises.

### SUFFERING WON'T LAST FOREVER

What is your responsibility? Trust God. Don't ever give up on God. Don't ever stop communicating with your Heavenly Father. He wants to fellowship with you. He wants to give you the instructions and plans for your life. He wants to restore the joy that you once had. He wants you to have sweet, peaceful sleep at night. He wants you to look forward to waking up in the morning. He loves you and cares about every thing in your life. Trust Him.

**So keep a firm grip on the faith. The suffering won't last forever. It won't be long**

**before this generous God who has great plans for us in Christ – eternal and glorious plans they are! – will have you put together again and on your feet for good. He gets the last word; yes, he does.**

– 1 Peter 5:9
The Message Bible

God gets the last word! Your days of sorrow are over. Your days of sadness are finished. Your sleepless nights have come to an end. Your responsibility is to **trust God.** How do you trust God? Read His Word. Get familiar with His promises for your life. You'll discover how much He truly loves you, cares about every detail of your life and wants to deliver you from all your trouble.

Spend time with Him in prayer every single day as if your life depends on it. Because it does. Worship and praise Him first thing in the morning. Confess the promises in this book out loud several times a day until they are so real in you that no one can convince you otherwise. Take it all in stride. God knows what He is doing and He is going to keep doing it until you are free!

## CONFESSION

*May your unfailing love be my comfort. . .*

– Psalm 119:76 (NIV)

*. . .My grace is sufficient for thee: for my strength is made perfect in weakness.*

– 2 Corinthians 12:9

*The righteous cry out, and the Lord hears them; he delivers them from all their troubles. The Lord is close to the brokenhearted and saves those who are crushed in spirit.*

– Psalm 34:17-18 (NIV)

*I sought the Lord, and he heard me, and delivered me from all my fears.*

– Psalm 34:4

# Chapter 3

# 3

## Arise from this Depression

Have you been under attack for a long time? Does there appear to be no let up for you? Are you never able to relax for a moment? When you are faced with a constant threat of hopelessness, failure and defeat, the pressure seems almost more than you can bear and depression sets in. If you are saying, "I don't know if I can take anymore," then, keep reading. You are a candidate for a refreshing.

Satan has tried his best to bring depression and discouragement to many of God's people, and in many cases, he has succeeded. There are many members of the body of Christ who are discouraged. They are depressed. They do not know where to turn. They do not know what to do. They don't know what they believe anymore.

There has been, in some cases, a falling away. People are going back into the world.

People are going back into their old lifestyles. They are disappointed. They are upset with God when God had nothing to do with it. God had nothing to do with throwing the three Hebrew children into the fiery furnace, but He had everything to do with bringing them out. God has nothing to do with the attacks that are on your life, but He will have everything to do with delivering you and setting you free!

That's something to smile about.

**Arise, Shine; for thy light is come, and the glory of the Lord is risen upon thee.**

– Isaiah 60:1

**Arise [from the depression and prostration in which circumstances have kept you – rise to a new life]! . . .**

– The Amplified Bible

***Depression*** is defined as *despair, sadness, gloominess, misery, hopelessness.* When you allow yourself to be depressed, you are declaring that there is no hope. When people allow themselves to fall into depression, they think they have no control over it. They can't control the tears. They can't control the circumstances. Those are lies from Satan to keep you depressed. I'm here to tell you that there is hope for your life and your circumstances. The Bible is our guide by which to live, and here is what God promises you.

**Then they cried out to the Lord in their trouble, and He saved them out of their distresses. He brought them out of darkness and the shadow of death, and broke their chains in pieces.**

– Psalm 107:13-14
The New King James Version

There's a promise from God that He hears your cries and He will deliver you, comfort you, restore you and heal your life! I encourage you to read that scripture out loud every day. Declare that promise in the face of your adversity. Let Satan hear what you believe. The Word says that God's Word does not return unto Him void, so stand on it (Isaiah 55:11)! He will deliver you from this depression. He will bring you out of this darkness.

Many people associate depression with darkness. They think of someone depressed as sitting in a room in the dark or laying in bed all day with the curtains drawn, no light coming in whatsoever. Satan represents the prince of darkness and God is the Father of Light. Psalm 107 just revealed that God will bring you out of darkness and the shadow of death and break your chains into pieces! It's time to shine some light on that dark outlook you've had on your life.

What do you do when you're depressed? How do you look beyond your seemingly hopeless situation and remain positive? Let's see what needs to be done first.

**Repent ye therefore, and be converted, that your sins may be blotted out, when the times of refreshing shall come from the presence of the Lord.**

– Acts 3:19

When you're facing depression, you desperately need a ***refreshing.*** How do you obtain a refreshing? The Word tells us to **repent.** What does ***repent*** mean? It means *to turn away from* *and go in the opposite direction.* Do you have unconfessed sin in your life? If so, don't go another day without getting on your knees and asking God to forgive you for the wrong choices and wrong thoughts that you've had.

The longer you go with unconfessed sin, the worse you feel about yourself which leads to depression which leads to distancing yourself from God. Don't fall into that trap. Repent. Get it behind you. Go in the opposite direction. Get rid of the sin in your life. Your life is too valuable to allow Satan to deceive you and destroy the plan of God for you.

**If we say that we have no sin, we deceive ourselves, and the truth is not in us. If we confess our sins, he is faithful and just to forgive us our sins, and to cleanse us from all unrighteousness.**

– 1 John 1:8-9

Unconfessed sin is like carrying a heavy load of luggage on your shoulders everywhere you go. It pulls you down, weighs you down, tires you out and eventually, you just can't go anymore. There's a freedom that comes once you've repented of the sin, asked God to forgive you and then go in the opposite direction.

Notice Acts 3:19 said, after you repent, times of refreshing will come. It is ***"times"*** of refreshing. It is not ***a*** time, singular. If it was ***a*** time, then that means it would be one event on God's agenda, and who knows if it may have already come and gone. But it is ***times*** of refreshing, plural, meaning it can happen more than once. It can happen from time to time. It can happen right now.

### AHHH...HOW REFRESHING!

The Amplified Bible describes this time of refreshing as **. . . (recovering from the effects of heat, or reviving with fresh air) may come from the presence of the Lord.**

Refreshing is a reviving, and a recovering. ***Recovering*** is defined as *an act of regaining, retaking or obtaining possession of anything which was lost or stolen.* That simply means that you are about to recover everything you lost during this attack and during this season of tribulation. Have you lost some sleep? You're going to gain it back. Have you lost your joy? Your peace? Your finances? Whatever you've lost is going to be regained.

Let me remind you that what you are experiencing is temporary. It is only a season of tribulation, and seasons change. They do not last forever. It may appear that it will last forever. You may think there is no end to this pain and misery, but seasons change. Satan is not going to be able to hold on to or keep back what he has stolen from you.

God is working behind the scenes even as you read this book. God is doing some miraculous things. God is moving by His Spirit. He is not going to allow you to stay in this state. He is not going to allow you to be beaten down, discouraged, depressed and wondering every day when will it all be over. God is moving right now, but you have to believe it. Your job is to **repent** and **get in the presence of the Lord.** If you will flow with God, then you will begin to experience a fresh infusion of Holy Ghost power. Your hope will be restored. Your faith will be energized, and all that has been stolen from you will come back into your hands!

Many of God's people today are in desperate need of a refreshing. Everywhere I go, I see it. The phone calls that we receive at our headquarters indicate that people all over the world are desperate for a breakthrough. I received a phone call recently from a minister and his wife who were in desperate need of new life. Their marriage was on the rocks. Then, the next day, I received another phone call from another minister and his wife who were in desperate need of new life. Their marriage was also on the rocks.

The body of Christ has been under a tremendous attack, but praise God, we are still standing. "Don't count us out yet, devil. We might get knocked down a time or two but we believe that when we fall, we shall arise" (Micah 7:8).

### WAITING FOR PERFECT CONDITIONS?

Times of refreshing are available to you, but you can't just sit back and wait for them. You have to thrust yourself into it. You can't just wait for some lightening bolt from heaven. You can't wait for your hair to stand up on the back of your neck. You have to reach for it.

The people who are experiencing freedom from oppression and depression are the people who have said, "I am going to get into this no matter what the devil says, no matter what is going on in my life. I don't care if my needs are not met yet. I don't care if I am under pressure. I don't care what it looks like. I am going all out for God."

If you say, "Well, as soon as I get back on my feet financially, I am going to get more serious about my relationship with God," it is unlikely that you will ever experience this refreshing and recovery. You can't wait until all the conditions are perfect. You have to start where you are. Start with what you've got. What *have* you got? Your mouth! Begin with confessing your sin, then speak faith-filled words over your life. Begin praising God with your mouth.

God inhabits the praises of His people. He resides, dwells in and abides in your midst when you praise Him. The most powerful weapon you have is your mouth. The most effective thing you can do with your mouth is **praise God.**

***"Why, Brother Jerry? Why should I praise God? Look at me. Look at my life!"***

Why? Because you serve the God of this Universe who created you to praise Him. He has wonderful plans for your life. He is the only One who can deliver you, heal you, pick you up and restore your life. You've got nothing to lose by praising God and everything to gain by doing it. So, why not do it! It's amazing what happens in the spirit realm when a child of God who's going through a treacherous storm raises his hands to heaven and says, "I praise You, Jesus. I worship You. I magnify You in my life. I worship You today. Thank You for turning this situation around." It confuses Satan more than anything else. He expects you to put your head down, stay in darkness and cry all day. The last thing he expects you to do is raise your head and your hands towards heaven and praise God.

When you praise God in your storm, (not ***for*** your storm), you are shutting Satan up. You are confusing the enemy. He doesn't know what to do. You are giving God something to work with. Just keep praising God until you sense the oppression leave. You will know it. It will seem as though the heaviness on your shoulders has been lifted off. Keep on praising God until you sense that freedom. It will come. But don't let it be a one-time thing. Praise God all day, every-day, throughout the day.

**This book of the law shall not depart out of thy mouth; but thou shalt meditate therein *day* and *night*, that thou mayest observe to do according to all that is written therein: for then thou shalt make thy way prosperous, and then thou shalt have good success.**

– Joshua 1:8

You have to be consistent in your praise and worship. God is looking for consistency. How badly do you want to be free? How badly do you want joy in your heart again? How badly do you want to wake up with a smile on your face? Then, get serious about improving your present condition by guarding <u>every</u> word that comes out of your mouth by the standard in God's Word. If it doesn't line up with the Word, don't speak it. Use your weapon (your mouth) to defeat Satan. Praise God consistently every day . . . day and night.

## DON'T WORRY, BE HAPPY

I was invited to a ministerial conference a few years ago, and the committee, who was in charge of this conference, told me what they wanted me to preach, which is something I don't normally agree to. But when they told me the subject they wanted me to discuss, I thought it was good. The letter read "Please, Brother Jerry, explain to us this strange phenomenon in the church. People are happy again. This joy, this laughter that is breaking out; what meaneth this?"

I was delighted to teach on that subject. My opening remarks in that meeting were, "You think it is strange that the church has joy. I think it is strange when the church has no joy. You think it is strange when people are laughing. I think it is strange when God's people are not. My Bible says, **. . . happy is that people, . . . whose God is the Lord** (Psalm 144:15). We ought to be the happiest people on the planet. You think it is strange when all of a sudden in the middle of a service, laughter breaks out. I don't think it is strange: I think it is the norm when the Holy Ghost is moving and reviving His people.

This is a time of refreshing, but you have got to get into it. You can't just sit back and wait for it. You have got to thrust yourself into it, cast all caution to the wind and go for it."

Even in the midst of trials, tribulations, pressure and attacks, perhaps like you have never experienced before, you are a candidate for a refreshing.

### Trade in Your Sorrow

Joy is a sign that God is in the house. Joy is a sign that new life is coming to you. Joy is a sign that a breakthrough is on the horizon.

**. . . weeping may endure for a night, but joy cometh in the morning.**

– Psalm 30:5

You may have had your nights of weeping, nights of sorrow, nights of pressure and discouragement, but thank God, joy comes in the morning. It is time to go all out for God and refuse to allow the devil to rob you of this wonderful visitation of the Lord. God wants to give you new life.

Are you ready for a breakthrough in your life?

**O give thanks unto the Lord; . . .sing unto him, sing psalms unto him: *talk* ye of all his wondrous works. He hath remembered his covenant for ever, the word which he commanded to a thousand generations. *And he brought forth his people with joy, and his chosen with gladness.***

– Psalm 105:1, 2, 8 and 43

Joy and gladness are signs of restoration; signs of new life. That is what God was doing when He brought the people out of Egypt. He brought them out with a strong hand. He brought them out with joy and gladness.

**He brought them forth also with silver and gold . . .**

– Psalm 105:37

Notice He not only gave them new life, but He restored to them what was rightfully theirs. They experienced a refreshing and a reviving but also recovery. You are headed for recovery.

You may feel like your situation is hopeless. You may go dragging into Church on Sunday morning saying, "Dear God, you don't know the trouble I have seen. I have been through the fire, Brother Jerry. Oh, dear God, did the devil visit our house this week!" But you are still here. You made it. And now it is recovery time! **Recovery** means you get everything back that was stolen from you. It means you *lay hold upon; retake, regain; and obtain possession of everything that rightfully belongs to you. It is recovery time.*

Throughout the Word of God, after God's people have experienced a season of refreshing, then comes their recovery, next comes their restoration, then comes the harvest for which they had been believing God.

Ask yourself right now, "How badly do I want recovery in my life? How badly do I want freedom from depression and oppression?" If you want it badly enough, then get your spiritual life right. Determine right now that you are going to press into God. Devote more time to fellowship and prayer. Completely surrender your will to His. Don't sit back and watch it happen to everyone else. Get in on it. Get out of your boat of depression, and get out on the water of refreshing.

Arise from this depression that has kept you back and kept you down. It is time to arise to new life. It is refreshing time in your life. It is restoration time. It is reviving time. It is recovery time. God does not want you to miss out on what He has planned for you. Be determined in Jesus' name that you are going to get right in the midst of it.

## CONFESSION

*Let the words of my mouth,*
*and the meditation of my heart,*
*be acceptable in thy sight,*
*O Lord, my strength and my redeemer.*

– Psalm 19:14

*Many are the afflictions of the*
*righteous: but the Lord delivereth*
*him out of them all.*

– Psalm 34:19

*. . . I will make darkness light before*
*them, and crooked things straight.*
*These things will I do unto them,*
*and not forsake them.*

– Isaiah 42:16

*Arise, shine; For your light has come!*
*And the glory of the*
*Lord is risen upon you.*

– Isaiah 60:1 (NKJ)

# Chapter 4

# 4

## The Road to Recovery

You have learned up to this point the way for you to experience freedom from oppression and get on the road to recovery in your life is to:

#1. Trust God.
#2. Repent.
#3. Don't give up.
#4. Praise God.

Now let's go a little deeper and see if anything else is missing in your life that could help you on your road to recovery.

In Lamentations 5:1, the people were crying out saying, **Remember, O Lord, what is come upon us: consider, and behold our reproach.** Trouble had come from all sides. They were distraught, miserable, and feeling hopeless. They were feeling like we have felt many times wondering if God really sees how bad things really are. Verse 15 says, **The joy of our heart is ceased . . .**

It is a sad thing when you reach the point in your life when the joy of your heart is ceased. ***Cease*** is defined as *to stop, finish, come to an end, come to a close, terminate, die down, die away or conclude.* I would never want to accept a life where joy has completely died away, concluded and come to an end. Your joy is something that you must protect at all times.

To me, having no joy is the absolute worst condition any person could ever find themselves in. It's one thing when you're discouraged. It's one thing when you feel like you can't stand anymore. But when joy has ceased, that's a pitiful state.

You may be thinking, *"That's easy for you to say, Brother Jerry. You can't even comprehend what I've been through. You wouldn't have any joy either if you'd had my life!"* Well, let's discover what true joy is from the Word of God.

### JOY VS. HAPPINESS

The Apostle Paul was able to keep his joy in the most trying of circumstances. When you read that man's life, it makes you think, *Dear God, what I'm going through is small compared to what this man went through.* He proved that joy is not based on circumstances. Joy is not some emotional roller coaster that will exalt you one moment and desert you the next.

Happiness is not like joy. Happiness is based on *happenings.* We allow circumstances to dictate whether we will be happy or sad. When things are going good, we are happy. When they aren't so good, we get sad.

Joy is a fruit of the spirit. It's just like faith. It's born in your spirit. It was placed there by God when you were born again. Jesus said, . . . **but now ask and keep asking and you will receive, so that your joy (gladness, delight) may be full and complete** (John 16:24 - Amplified translation). Jesus expects us to be full of joy no matter what we go through. Joy is a spiritual force that resides on the inside of you no matter what your circumstances are. It can sustain you through the most severe storms.

The reason Paul had this tremendous joy was not because everything was going well for him. Some Christians are only joyful when everything is going well. Paul's joy was not based on his circumstances. His joy was a product of his intimate relationship with Jesus. His relationship with Jesus brought more joy to his life than anything else in the world. Of course, he tells us that his ultimate goal, even though he knew Jesus well, was that he might know Him more. Well, if he had this kind of joy with the relationship that he already had, what do you suppose would happen to his joy if he got to know Jesus more? The same thing can happen to you. He writes this letter encouraging every believer to tap into this joy that can only come from *knowing Jesus.*

In other words, we learn from Paul that spending time with Jesus will produce joy in our lives. The Word says in Psalm 16:11 **. . . in thy presence is fulness of joy . . .** The more time you devote in prayer, praise and worship, the more joy you will have.

**Finally, my brethren, rejoice in the Lord . . .**

– Philippians 3:1

**. . . delight yourself in the Lord and continue to rejoice that you are in Him . . .**

– The Amplified Bible

No matter what might come your way, no matter what challenges you're facing today, nothing can change the fact that you are in Him and He is in you. It is a great joy to know that you are in Christ and Christ is in you.

Paul tells us in Philippians 4:13 - **I can do all things through Christ which strengtheneth me.** Because we are in Christ and He is in us, we can do **all** things through Him that strengthens us. Not only can we do all things, but we can overcome all things *through Him.*

As you read the story of Paul's life, it becomes very clear that Paul's joy was irrepressible. You could not stop this man's joy no matter what he went through. They beat him and he was joyful. They put him in chains and he was joyful. They locked him in a prison and he remained joyful. They thought they had finally shut the man up, and at midnight, he broke out into singing. You couldn't stop the man's joy. It appears that his joy was constant even when he was suffering and even when he was experiencing uncomfortable conditions.

Many times, when we refer to Paul, we mention Paul's faith. We know that he was a great man of faith. But I believe that there is another characteristic about this man's life that should be mentioned right alongside his faith, and that is his joy.

The people in Lamentations had lost many things. They had lost many possessions, confidence, stability, security, peace, and most of all, joy. They didn't see anything in their lives to be joyful about.

**Turn thou us unto thee, O Lord, and we shall be turned; renew our days as of old.**

– Lamentations 5:21

What were they saying? In other words, "God, we need some restoration in our lives. We've lost many things. There are many negative things happening in our lives. There is nothing positive that we can point at. And we've lost our joy. Our joy has withered away. Restore us, Lord" (Author's paraphrase).

## Joy In Adversity

Have you recently asked God for some restoration? Many times, we find ourselves needing restoration. Why? Because Satan is a thief. He comes to steal, to kill and to destroy your life (John 10:10). I'm sure he's stolen some things from you. He may have stolen your marriage, your finances, your children, your job, your peace, your joy, your confidence. He is a thief out to destroy your life. And what you need is restoration.

You may be waking up in the middle of the night wondering where in the world you are going to get the money to meet that need. *God, is it over? Is this as far as we go? What did I do to get into this kind of condition? God, have I sinned? Lord, what is going on here?* The worst thing you can do is lose your joy. Joy is vitally important in the midst of adversity. Joy is a **powerful** force.

**But call to remembrance the former days, in which, after ye were illuminated, ye endured a great fight of afflictions; Partly, whilst ye were made a gazingstock both by reproaches and afflictions; and partly, whilst ye became companions of them that were so used.**

**For ye had compassion of me in my bonds, and took joyfully the spoiling of your goods, knowing in yourselves that ye have in heaven a better and an enduring substance.**

– Hebrews 10:32-34

Many years ago, the Spirit of God said to me, "The most important thing for you to do when Satan is trying to take everything you've got is **maintain your joy.** Don't ever let him steal your joy." I wrote a book entitled, If Satan Can't Steal Your Joy, He Can't Keep Your Goods, and it has literally gone around the world restoring joy to the hopeless. The joy of the Lord is your strength (Nehemiah 8:10). What you need most in the middle of a storm is strength to carry on. The Lord explained it to me this way: "If you have no joy, you have no strength. If you have no strength, then you can't resist. If you can't resist, then the devil will not flee. And if the devil doesn't flee, then you will not win." Your victory is directly linked to your joy.

**Restore unto me the joy of my salvation . . .**

– Psalm 51:12

Apparently, the Psalmist had lost that joy. It's obvious why, because of all of the adversity and the challenges that he faced. David was a man who was certainly familiar with challenges and adversity. He lost many things. Sometimes joy is the only thing you have left to hold onto. You don't have the money. You don't have the resources. You don't have the wisdom. You don't have the ability, but if you have joy, then there's still a chance to beat the devil at his own game. Never lose your joy.

## Rejoice . . . When?

**Rejoice in the Lord always: and again I say, Rejoice.**

– Philippians 4:4

When should you rejoice? Always.

"What about this storm I'm going through?" That comes under the category of *always.*

"Yea, but I'm hurting. I'm miserable. I'm depressed." That still comes under the category of *always.* He didn't say, "Rejoice because nothing is working." Or, "Rejoice because your body is under attack." Or, "Rejoice because you don't have enough money and your spouse left you." He was saying to rejoice <u>in</u> those circumstances not <u>for</u> them.

You are not thanking God *for* the trials. God is not the author of trials. You are praising God in the midst of trials and adversity. You praise God anyway. You praise God and rejoice because you know that your God is turning things around. You know that this pain and this adversity is only temporary. Your freedom is on the horizon. You are confusing the devil and causing him to lose his grip on your life when you begin praising God.

### No More Anxiety

**Be careful for nothing; but in every thing by prayer and supplication with thanksgiving let your requests be made known unto God.**

– Philippians 4:6

**Do not fret or have any anxiety about anything . . .**

– The Amplified Bible

Are you full of anxiety? Are you frustrated? Are you worried? Are you wondering how you are going to get out of this? Are you on the verge of losing all of your joy? Keep reading. Your answers are right there in the Word of God.

**. . . I therein do rejoice, yea, and will *rejoice*. For I know that this shall turn to my**

**salvation through your prayer, and the supply of the Spirit of Jesus Christ.**

– Philippians 1:18-19

The letter the Apostle Paul wrote to the Philippian church was probably the happiest, most joyful letter he ever wrote. He wrote that letter when he was in jail and facing death. You could say he was on death row. Yet, he writes the most joyful letter that he ever wrote. In fact, you'll find the words joy and rejoicing both in their noun and verb forms at least 16 times in four chapters in the epistle to the Philippian church. When you see joy or rejoicing 16 times in four chapters that should tell you something. He's trying to get a message to us. It seems that Paul's primary goal in writing this letter to the church at Philippi was to encourage the believers there to avoid becoming faint-hearted when facing adversity, trials and tribulations.

He was reminding them of the importance of remaining true to their faith in God no matter what kind of circumstances they may face. They knew that Paul was in jail when he wrote this letter. They knew that he was facing death. Paul was saying, "I'm still rejoicing. And if I can rejoice in my circumstances, you can rejoice in yours" (Author's paraphrase).

You may be facing some of the toughest times you've ever experienced in your life right now; but let me remind you, you probably have more to be thankful for than Paul did. Above all, you have promises from God that He will never leave you nor forsake you. That alone should bring a smile. That should brighten your eyes.

**The righteous cry, and the Lord heareth, and delivereth them out of all their troubles. The Lord is nigh unto them that are of a broken heart; and saveth such as be of a contrite spirit.**

– Psalm 34:17-18

**When I said, My foot slippeth; thy mercy, O Lord, held me up. In the multitude of my thoughts within me thy comforts delight my soul.**

– Psalm 94:18-19

The comfort of God will restore your soul and bring joy back into your life.

## Get In Position For Victory

Paul was urging us to stay in faith and joy. With those two components, you can defeat Satan and come out of this storm on top!

**And in nothing terrified by your adversaries: which is to them an evident token of perdition, but to you of salvation, and that of God.**

– Philippians 1:28

He was saying that you don't have to be terrified by your adversary. You don't have to give in to his tactics. You don't have to give up just because it looks as though defeat is inevitable. He assured us that if we will maintain our joy and not give in, then what God started in us, He will complete.

**Being confident of this very thing, that he which hath begun a good work in you will perform it until the day of Jesus Christ . . .**

– Philippians 1:6

I believe that if you can maintain your joy even when it looks like what you are facing is impossible, then it will cause you to possess the courage of a lion. It will enable you to stand no matter what you are going through. It will enable you to position yourself for some of the greatest victories you have ever experienced in your life. This is not an easy thing to do. It is a challenge. But you don't have to fight this battle alone. The Greater One is on the inside of you and will enable you to overcome every obstacle.

### PEACE IS YOURS

**Therefore, my brethren dearly beloved and longed for, my joy and crown, so stand fast in the Lord, my dearly beloved. And the peace of God, which passeth all understanding, shall keep your hearts and minds through Christ Jesus.**

– Philippians 4:1,7

If you will not give up in this adversity and pressure you're experiencing, there will come a peace in your life that is beyond anything you can understand. God will cause you to rest in Him.

What else do you need when you are facing a trial if you have joy, you have courage, you have faith and you have peace? Those spiritual forces will get you over! There is no way that you can lose when these spiritual forces are present in your life.

## God Is Your Defense

**But let all those that put their trust in thee rejoice: . . . because thou defendest them . . .**

– Psalm 5:11

We should rejoice because we have this promise. God is defending us. He is our defense. The Amplified Bible says that **he will make a covering over us.** That doesn't mean that Satan won't attack us. He will attack, but if we maintain our joy; Satan will not be able to penetrate that covering. Thank God we know that He is on our side defending us.

I like to say what Paul said, . . . **If God be for us, who can be against us?** (Romans 8:31). It's only when we allow ourselves to become like the people in Lamentations where the joy of their hearts had ceased, that we get into big trouble. When you have no joy, you are headed for defeat. But if you make up your mind that you are not going to let these things rob you of your joy, then there is still hope for victory.

Again, how do you obtain joy when every thing in your life seems to be falling apart? On your knees in the presence of the Lord. Spending time praising God brings supernatural joy to your life like you've never experienced before.

### SELF-TALK

**And my soul shall be joyful in the Lord . . .**

– Psalm 35:9

There are times when you just have to demand yourself to be joyful even when you don't feel like it. There are times when you need to just pull yourself in front of a mirror, point your finger at yourself and say, "You are not going to let this rob you of your joy. Jesus is still Lord. God is still on His throne. The Word still works. The Name of Jesus is still the most powerful thing in this Universe, and you are not going to give up as long as you know these things."

The Psalmist talked to himself. I've had people say, "I'm a little leery of those people who talk to themselves." I'm a little concerned about people who don't, because sometimes you **have** to talk to yourself. You have to say - "Soul, you will be joyful. Soul, you will rejoice. Soul, you are not going to be down today. I realize it looks like there is nothing working, but something is working behind the scenes. God is working. The angels are working. The Holy Ghost is working and I've got a reason to shout this morning, praise God." You can talk yourself into being joyful.

You cannot put a price on the value of joy that is maintained in the midst of adversity. You have to let the devil know that you still have your joy, and there isn't anything that he can do to steal if from you. I dare you to show him today!

## Everything Stolen Will Be Returned

What have you lost during this storm? Count it all up. Have you lost your position? Have you lost some years? Have you lost some finances? What has Satan stolen from you? When Satan has done his best to take everything you have, but you still maintain your joy, then God promises restoration. You will get it back. Hallelujah. God will not allow the devil to keep it. You will either get back what was stolen or God will bless you with better.

**The voice of joy, and the voice of gladness, the voice of the bridegroom, and the voice of the bride, the voice of them that shall say, Praise the Lord of hosts: for the Lord is good; for his mercy endureth for ever: and of them that shall bring the sacrifice of praise into the house of the Lord. For I will cause to return the captivity of the land, as at the first, saith the Lord.**

– Jeremiah 33:11

God is saying that if you'll give voice to joy in the midst of adversity, He will turn your captivity. He will reverse your circumstance and return what has been stolen.

Maintaining your joy in adversity is not the easiest thing in the world to do. I'm not insinuating that it is. It takes determination. It takes a quality decision. It takes a lot of determination. But you have to ask yourself, "How much is restoration worth? Is it worth the effort?" I believe it is.

I want to challenge you today that if you're going through some tough times, and you've been having some sleepless nights wondering how in the world you are going to get out of this situation you're in, then settle it in your heart right now that nothing is going to steal your joy. Settle it in your heart right now that you are going to rejoice in the Lord no matter how impossible your situation looks. Settle it in your heart right now that you're going to praise the Lord even if it gets worse after today. Satan is not going to get you down. Settle it in your heart that once and for all, you are going to stay focused and not give up on your dream. Don't give up on your vision of freedom in every area of your life. The joy of the Lord is your strength to defeat oppression.

## CONFESSION

*Thou wilt show me the path of life: in thy presence is fulness of joy; at thy right hand there are pleasures for evermore.*
– Psalm 16:11

*I can do all things through Christ which strengtheneth me.*
– Philippians 4:13

*Restore unto me the joy of thy salvation; and uphold me with thy free spirit.*
– Psalm 51:12

*For I know that this shall turn to my salvation through your prayer, and the supply of the Spirit of Jesus Christ.*
– Philippians 1:19

*The righteous cry, and the Lord heareth, and delivereth them out of all their troubles. The Lord is nigh unto them that are of a broken heart; and saveth such as be of a contrite spirit.*
– Psalm 34:17-18

# Chapter 5

# 5

## Free At Last

When the Lord gave me the messages on freedom, I discovered that ***freedom*** is defined as *the state of being exempt from the control of another.* The opposite of freedom is bondage. ***Bondage*** is defined *as subjection to captivity or restraint.* If you've been a slave to the bondage of oppression and depression, then today is your day to decree that you are free . . . at last.

Can you imagine someone walking into a prison and saying, "I have come to announce today that you are free?" What do you think would happen in that place? "Oh, thank you, let me get my bag." I don't think so. I think there would be a riot.

If somebody walked into the finest hospital in your city and announced to every person who was sick, diseased, dying of incurable diseases: "I have come to announce to you today that you are healed. You are free. Go home and live a normal life." What kind of response do you think you would hear from those people? Shouting, dancing, screaming, jumping . . . excitement everywhere!

Yet, we read passages from the Bible that clearly declare that we don't have to live oppressed and miserable, we are free in Jesus, and what do we say? "Oh, let's see what else I can find."

### Wardrobe Change

**The Spirit of the Lord God is upon me; because the Lord hath anointed me to preach good tidings unto the meek; he hath sent me to bind up the brokenhearted, to proclaim liberty to the captives, and the opening of prison to them that are bound; To proclaim the acceptable year of the Lord, and the day of vengeance of our God; to comfort all that mourn;**

**To appoint unto them that mourn in Zion, to give unto them beauty for ashes, the oil of joy for mourning, the garment of praise**

**for the spirit of heaviness; that they might be called the trees of righteousness, the planting of the Lord, that he might be glorified.**

– Isaiah 61:1-3

Jesus came to announce **<u>your freedom.</u>** He came to proclaim freedom to every captive of oppression, depression, loneliness, hopelessness, misery, etc. That includes you. . . today. Notice that it says, "He changed their mourning to comfort." He will comfort you. He will change your mourning to joy. He will give you the garment of praise for the spirit of heaviness. Apparently, these words ***spirit*** and ***garment*** are interchangeable in this verse because when the spirit of heaviness is on you, you wear it like a coat. If you see a person who has oppression and heaviness on them, it is as if they are wearing a garment of heaviness. It weighs them down. Jesus was saying, "I am going to redress you. I am going to change your attire. I am going to take off that old garment of heaviness, and I am going to put on you the new garment of praise" (Author's paraphrase).

Once Jesus puts this garment of praise on you, He expects you to wear it all the time. . . not just when it is time to go to church, not just when things are going well, not just when there's peace in your home and marriage, not just when you have all the money you need . . . but all the time.

Stop changing your garment during the week. At church, while you are singing you have your garment of praise on, but then you go home and begin looking around at everything, all the bills, all the problems and you say, "Well, I guess I better take my garment of praise off and put on my garment of heaviness."

That garment of heaviness fits real good. It's just your size. Satan will tailor-make you a garment of heaviness. He makes it fit perfect; not too tight, not too baggy. It's your color. And it feels right. The reason we are uncomfortable wearing the garment of praise is because it is Jesus' coat, and sometimes it doesn't fit us well. Why? Because we've become more used to the old garment of heaviness. It was made for us. It fits perfectly. That is the one we're used to wearing all the time.

Do you have a pair of jeans or a jogging suit that you enjoy wearing when you get home? It's comfortable. You enjoy lounging around the house in them. It feels good. It's not tight around your waist. It has an *elastic* waist so you can eat whatever you want to eat, and it won't get too tight. But then when it's time to go to work, you dress up. You put those uncomfortable shoes on, those pants that are a little snug around the waist, then you add a belt on top of that! You would much rather wear your jogging suit, but you can't wear that to work. It's not part of the dress code. Everyone would notice you weren't abiding by the rules. So, you endure all day at work, but as soon as you get home . . . ahhh . . . lounge clothes again!

Well, we do the same thing in the spirit realm. We wear that old garment of heaviness that fits us just perfectly at home. We complain all week about our problems, our situation, our failing marriage, our lack of finances. We cry, we worry, we allow oppression to come on us. But then about 9:30 a.m. on Sunday morning, we say, "Oh, it is time for church. Let me put that garment of praise on. Oh hallelujah.

Hallelujah." It's uncomfortable, but we can endure it for a few hours at church. After all, it's part of the *dress code.* Everyone would notice if we weren't abiding by the *rules* and wearing the garment of heaviness to church. You just don't do that at church.

We go to church, sing praise and worship, and suddenly, while we are praising God with our hands lifted up, it starts fitting better. We're not so uncomfortable anymore. In fact, it feels light. It feels free. It feels good.

Then we get in our cars and drive home. Our spouse says, "Well, you know, it was tough last week. I might get laid off. There are a lot of people down at our place getting laid off. I don't know what we are going to do, sweetheart. If I get laid off, we can't make it." Then, you say, "Before we continue this conversation, let me get my garment of heaviness on. Oh woe is us. Woe is us. Dear God, what are we going to do? We will probably lose everything we've got. I don't know why this always happens to us."

"What did you say, sweetheart? It's Wednesday night. Time to go to church? Let me change my clothes!"

It is time that we get rid of that garment of heaviness and start wearing the garment of praise until it fits. Just keep it on until it fits; until it is tailor-made for you. When you truly have a revelation of what Jesus did at Calvary, that heaviness will not stay on you. I don't care what you are going through. I don't care how bad it gets. You will praise God anyway. No matter what they are saying on TV, you praise God. No matter what kind of mail you get tomorrow, you praise God anyway. No matter what your bank statement says, you praise God anyway. No matter how ugly your spouse treats you, you praise God anyway.

I am not talking about pretending those situations don't exist. I am not suggesting that you just play like none of those things are really happening. I am saying that you don't let situations steal your joy, your faith and your hope, that it will turn around. You don't allow your circumstances to dictate what you wear! Don't allow situations to cause you to keep switching from the garment of praise to the garment of heaviness. You just keep your garment of praise on, regardless.

The devil may ask, "What are you shouting about?"

"Well, in case you haven't read, devil, Isaiah 53 says Jesus is my Deliverer. I'm free! I don't have to be oppressed any longer!" Then, just break forth into singing and cry aloud. You are free, but you have to enforce that freedom.

I want to encourage you right now to not give up until you are free in every area of your life. The Bible already says you are free, but now you are pressing for the manifestation of it in every area.

### Jesus Wants You Free

In Luke 4, we see Jesus fulfilling the prophetic word that Isaiah was speaking about. He declared that His primary mission would be to set mankind free. He said that Jesus would come proclaiming release for the captives and the acceptable year of the Lord.

**The Spirit of the Lord is upon me, because he hath anointed me to preach the gospel to the poor; he hath sent me to heal the brokenhearted, to preach deliverance to the captives, and recovering of sight to the blind, to *set at liberty* them that are bruised, to preach the acceptable year of the Lord.**

– Luke 4:18-19

Notice he was quoting Isaiah 61.

**. . . And when he had opened the book, he found the place where it was written,**

**The Spirit of the Lord is upon me, because he hath anointed me to preach the gospel to the poor; he hath sent me to heal the brokenhearted, to preach deliverance to the captives, and recovering of sight to the blind, to *set at liberty* them that are bruised,**

**To preach the acceptable year of the Lord. And he closed the book, and he gave it**

**again to the minister, and sat down. And the eyes of all them that were in the synagogue were fastened on him. And he began to say unto them, this day is the scripture fulfilled in your ears.**

– Luke 4:17-21

What was He saying? "The person that Isaiah was prophesying about is now in your midst. It's Me. I'm here now" (Author's paraphrase). I would have thought that everybody in that building would have jumped up and shouted and screamed and the whole town would have been filled with joy and laughter because the One that they had been waiting for had just declared that He was in their midst.

Instead of rejoicing, they wanted to kill him. They thought, *Who does he think he is? This is the carpenter's boy. We have known this man ever since he was born. He was raised in this synagogue. We know his father, his mother, his brothers and his sisters. Who does he think he is, coming in here and telling us that he is the one that Isaiah prophesied about?* (Author's paraphrase).

It made them so mad that they took Him outside to a cliff and tried to kill Him. Religious tradition is an awful thing. It makes the Word of God of no effect.

The Amplified Bible says that Jesus came to "announce release to the captives." The New International Version says, "to proclaim freedom." Jesus came to proclaim freedom to you and me. It was the theme of His ministry, and it is available to you right now in your life. But you can't be like those people in Luke who didn't grab hold of it. They didn't believe it. They denied the freedom that was right there waiting for them. Your freedom is here. It's already been paid for on the cross. You have to take hold of it.

## Fed Up With Bondage?

As we study Jesus' ministry, there is no doubt that God wants you to be totally free. The New International Version calls this "the year of the Lord's favor." Jesus came to announce that you are free and it is time for you to experience your freedom.

God established the acceptable year of the Lord or the year of God's favor. He established that way back in the history of the Israelites out of an act of His love and compassion towards them even though they didn't deserve it.

They had broken covenant with God. They rebelled. But God, in His compassion, did not want His people in bondage, even though they deserved bondage. He told them that if they kept the Book of the law, and did all that He commanded, then blessings would come on them and overtake them. But their rebellion caused them to get out from under the umbrella of protection and they became targets for the devil. Bondage was the result. They went into bondage to Egypt because of **disobedience** and **rebellion.** After a period of time, they finally got fed up with the bondage, and they cried out, "God help us. Please send us a deliverer. Do something."

Remember, bondage is defined as subjection to captivity or restraint.

## God Hears Your Cries

They began to cry out, and God heard their cry. He remembered His covenant, and sent Moses to deliver them out of that bondage. It wasn't long after God delivered them out of Egypt, that they were breaking covenant again. They were rebellious. They were disobedient. That same curse came on them, and they were in bondage again. Most of their lives they were in bondage.

You may have cried out to God and He delivered you, but then you found yourself back in the same boat of rebellion and disobedience again. You most likely, feel bondage in your life. Rebellion and disobedience will produce bondage and oppression. But thank God His mercy endures forever!

God hears your cries no matter how many times you mess up. He is rich in mercy. He will pick you up every time you call on His Name. He loves you. He wants the best for your life. He wants you free from this bondage.

Have you ever done something for your children when you know they didn't deserve it, but you did it anyway? Why? Because you love them. Sometimes I am told by my children, "Dad, don't buy the grandkids anything right now. They are in trouble." But then, when I see them, I can't help it. The next thing I know, I am buying the latest tennis shoes for all five of them! "Daddy, why did you do that?" I can't help it. I have been hanging around God too long. Maybe they don't deserve them right now, but I love them. These people in Lamentations didn't deserve God's favor, but what did God do? He poured His love and mercy on them any way.

God loves you, and He does not want you in bondage. Back in the Old Testament, He established what He called "the acceptable year of the Lord." That was one year of freedom. Can you imagine that? His best was for them to experience freedom every day of their lives; however, one year of freedom is better than no freedom at all.

## Go Blow Your Horn

**And thou shalt number seven sabbaths of years unto thee, seven times seven years; and the space of the seven sabbaths of years shall be unto thee forty and nine years. Then shalt thou cause the trumpet of the jubilee to sound on the tenth day of the seventh month . . .**

Now that is going into the fiftieth year.

**. . . the tenth day of the seventh month, in the day of atonement . . .**

– Leviticus 25:8-9

What does atonement represent? Release. Under the old covenant, they could only experience a covering of sins. But the blood of Jesus did not atone our sins, it destroyed them and wiped them away. Our sins haven't been covered, they have been remitted. Isn't that good news? You don't have to hold your head down in shame and guilt any longer. Once you've asked God to forgive you, repented of your sins, then it is washed away by the blood of Jesus . . . never to be remembered again. In other words, you are free from your past!

Under the Old Covenant, the blood of bulls and goats could never remit sin, they could only cover them for a year. Then they had to return and make the same sacrifice. Jesus doesn't have to come down from heaven every year and pay the price again; die and be raised again. Why? Because His blood did it **once and for all.**

**And ye shall hallow the fiftieth year, and proclaim liberty** (or freedom) **throughout all the land unto all the inhabitants thereof: it shall be a jubilee unto you; and ye shall return every man unto his possession, and ye shall return every man unto his family. A jubilee shall that fiftieth year be unto you . . .**

– Leviticus 25:10-11

A year of freedom!

It didn't matter what kind of bondage they were in, the moment that trumpet sounded, they were free. If they had been a slave, they were released. Whatever had been stolen from them, it was restored.

Just imagine if you had been in bondage, or you were a slave, and everything you had was taken from you, but you knew that as soon as the trumpet was blown, ***everything*** in your life would be drastically changed! You would declare: "Free at last, free at last! Thank God Almighty, I am free at last."

Can you image the jubilation? Can you imagine the excitement? Well, you should because that same freedom is available for you and me right now!

Every Israelite knew what Jubilee was about, but by the time Jesus came into His earthly ministry, their religious traditions had done away with Jubilee. However, they had heard their ancestors talk about it. They had read about it in the book of the prophets, but they were not enjoying it.

It's no wonder God told Isaiah that when this Redeemer comes, He will bring back Jubilee, but it is going to be a little different. He was saying to them: "I am bringing Jubilee back to mankind. But Jubilee will no longer be a space in time. Jubilee is now a person, and I am that person. I am your Jubilee. I am your freedom. I have come to announce that ***you are free***" (Author's paraphrase).

God still requires *horn blowing.* It is just done a little differently now. If you want to experience Jubilee, there has to be some horn blowing of your own. There has to be a trumpet sound. And it must be ***you!***

### Shout Your Freedom

"How, Brother Jerry? I've never played a horn before?"

You announce your freedom, not with a shofar, or with a musical instrument, but with the **words of your mouth.** That is how you blow your trumpet of freedom. The Bible says, **let the redeemed of the Lord say so** (Psalm 107:2).

### Praise Is Your Key

God was saying that when you are at the end of your rope, shout, the "mercy of God endures forever." You know, it could be that we are shouting the wrong things when we are at the end of our rope. It could be that we have been shouting the wrong things when we are in over our heads. We have been shouting the wrong things when our back is against the wall. We have been shouting, "Oh, I am dying. Get me out of here. Help! I am sinking." That is not what He told them to shout. If you are at the end of your rope today, maybe you need to start shouting, "Praise ye the Lord. For the Lord is good and His mercy endures forever."

## God Will Not Fail You

My wife, Carolyn, and I can testify to you that in thirty-four years of ministry and having faced impossible situations and often feeling like we were in over our heads, God has never failed us. He has NEVER failed us. Not one time.

I have reason to believe that if He hasn't done it over the last thirty-four years, then He is not going to do it in my future either. He is not going to fail you. Why? The Psalmist said, *you will answer me because You love me.* If for no other reason, He loves you. Even when you don't deserve it, He loves you anyway. His love and mercy can cause every circumstance in your life to be turned around for your good.

**O give thanks unto the Lord; for he is good: because his mercy endureth for ever. Let Israel now say, that his mercy endureth for ever. Let the house of Aaron now say, that his mercy endureth for ever.**

– Psalm 118:1-3

His mercy endures ***forever.*** His mercy is available for you right now, tomorrow, next week, next month. But you have to cry out for the mercy of God.

Notice what he says immediately after that (verse 5): **I called upon the Lord in distress: the Lord answered me, and set me in a large place.**

Many times, when you feel like you are in over your head, you can feel confined, restricted, compressed, and you think you have no space. There is nowhere to turn. David had a revelation of the mercy of God and he said, "Because I reverence Him and I fear Him and I respect Him, when I am in distress, when I am at the end of my rope, when I am in over my head, I can call unto Him. He answers me and He delivers me from my small place. And He moves me into a large place" (Author's paraphrase).

Verse 6 – **The Lord is on my side; I will not fear . . .** In verse 5 he says, **I called upon the Lord in distress.** The Message translation says, **pushed to the wall, I called to God . . .** In other words, when your back is against the wall and there is nowhere to turn, God will have mercy on you.

## God's Grace Is Sufficient For You

It makes no difference how you describe your situation, *pushed to the wall, end of your rope, in over your head* . . . God's mercy is enough. God's mercy is sufficient.

One commentary said, "Perhaps, there is no word in our English language that is precisely synonymous with the Hebrew word ***mercy;*** however, the closest word is ***grace***." Grace can be translated into ***favor.***

## Get Your Eyes On God

If you are in over your head, then you need to call on God for a favor. Say, "I need a favor today, Lord." The favor of God is sufficient for whatever you are going through. In the Old Testament, in particular, when God's people were facing impossible situations, they called on the mercy of God.

One example is found in Second Chronicles 20. Jehoshaphat, and the children of Israel, were totally out numbered by enemy forces. They had very little hope. So, what did they do? They lifted up their hands and said, "God, we don't know what to do, but our eyes are on You." They asked God for His mercy. What did God tell them to do? He told them to go and confront their enemies. He said to get the praisers and the singers out front and confront their enemies. He instructed them to stand in their presence and begin to say, "Praise ye the Lord. For the Lord is good and His mercy endureth forever."

That reveals to me that when you don't know what to do, then praise always comes first.

**Let the redeemed of the Lord say so, whom he hath redeemed from the hand of the enemy.**

– Psalm 107:2

Every time you declare your freedom, you are blowing a horn right in Satan's ears. The blowing of the trumpet in Leviticus was symbolic of making a decree. When they heard that trumpet sound, they were making a profound statement in the spirit decreeing their freedom.

**. . . the sword of the Spirit, which is the word of God.**

– Ephesians 6:17

Every time you speak the Word of God, it is a sword coming out of your mouth. It is a trumpet being blown. No wonder the devil fights us so hard about confessing the Word. Everything I have was obtained by confessing the Word of God. I am blowing my trumpet in the devil's face and telling him, "You are not keeping me poor. You are not keeping me sick. You are not keeping me broke. You are not taking my marriage. You are not taking my children. I am the redeemed and I am saying so." It is time for you to blow your horn of freedom.

**Thou shalt also decree a thing, and it shall be established unto thee. . .**

– Job 22:28

You are decreeing something when you speak God's Word. Every time you declare that as the redeemed of the Lord, the Son has made you free, it carries the same strength, the same weight, the same power as that man in Leviticus when he stood up on the seventh month, the tenth day, the forty-ninth year and he blew that shofar. Freedom is yours!

### You Are Free From Oppression

Have you ever been around someone who is learning to play a horn? It is annoying, to say the least. You can't concentrate on anything because that crazy horn is so loud. Well, you may not be proficient at declaring your freedom yet, so just drive the devil nuts with your *horn blowing.* When you get up in the morning, just say, "Satan, it is me again and I've got my horn!"

Begin praising God and shouting your freedom. Blow it all day. Blow it all night. Keep blowing your horn of freedom until the manifestation of that freedom comes into your life. Don't quit praising God. It is your weapon against oppression, depression, hopelessness, misery, torment, confusion. It is your answer. Praise God with the words of your mouth. Be proficient at it.

Keep blowing your horn by declaring the Word, confessing the scriptures, using your sword of the Spirit until every bondage and every yoke is destroyed in your life.

It is time for you to be free. It is time for you to have the yoke of bondage broken off of you. It is time to get well. It is time to get healed. It is time to prosper. It's time to have joy. It's time to get your marriage and family restored. Get your life back. Get your vision and your dreams back.

Your life is not over. Your best days are not behind you. Don't listen to Satan's lies. The best is yet to come. You are on your way to the greatest times of your life. Don't settle for your life as it is. Don't accept defeat and misery as final. Forget what's behind you. Remember it no more! It's over. It's called the past for a reason. It has passed! So, let it go. Repent, turn away from and go in the opposite direction. Seek God with all of your heart. Guard what you allow your mind to think on and your mouth to say. Be constantly conscious of what you're saying. Speak the Word of God by day and by night. Don't speak idle, negative, doubtful words. Consume your life with faith-building tapes playing daily. Freedom becomes more of a reality the more you talk about it. The more you vocalize your freedom, the more you cause spiritual laws to go to work in your behalf. Speak the Word. Speak the Word. Speak the Word. I can't say it enough!

Begin praising God. As soon as the depression tries to come on you, begin praising God over and over and over again until you sense that oppression has lifted. It will lift. Keep at it. Don't just try it for a week and if nothing changes, give up! Don't put this book down and say, "Ahhh . . . that was a nice, little book that Brother Jerry wrote." Get serious about changing the quality of your life. Get determined to be free from this oppression that Satan has put on you. It doesn't belong to you. Jesus paid an awesome price for your freedom. It's already yours. Now, go get it! I declare in the name of Jesus that you are free at last from oppression.

# CONFESSION

*For thou hast delivered my soul from death, mine eyes from tears, and my feet from falling. I will walk before the Lord in the land of the living.*

– Psalm 116:8-9

*I called upon the Lord in distress: the Lord answered me, and set me in a large place. The Lord is on my side; I will not fear: what can man do unto me?*

– Psalm 118:5-6

*Let the redeemed of the Lord say so, whom he hath redeemed from the hand of the enemy.*

– Psalm 107:2

*Thou shalt also decree a thing, and it shall be established unto thee: and the light shall shine upon thy ways.*

– Job 22:28

## About The Author

**Dr. Jerry Savelle** is a noted author, evangelist, pastor and teacher who travels extensively throughout the United States, Canada, and around the globe. He is president of Jerry Savelle Ministries International, a ministry of many outreaches devoted to meeting the needs of Believers all over the world.

Well-known for his balanced Biblical teaching, Dr. Savelle has conducted seminars, crusades and conventions for over thirty years as well as ministering in thousands of churches and fellowships. He is in great demand today because of his inspiring message of victory and faith and his vivid, and often humorous, illustrations from the Bible. He teaches the uncompromising Word of God with a power and an authority that is exciting, but with a love that delivers the message directly to the spirit man.

In addition to his international headquarters in Crowley, Texas, Dr. Savelle is also founder of JSMI-United Kingdom, JSMI-South Africa, JSMI-Asia, JSMI-Tanzania, JSMI-Australia and JSMI-Botswana. He established the Heritage of Faith Correspondence School, and also pastors a church with his wife, Carolyn, in Crowley, Texas, called Heritage of Faith Christian Center.

The missions outreaches of his ministry extend to over 50 countries around the world.

Dr. Savelle has written many books and has an extensive video and cassette teaching tape ministry and a nation-wide television broadcast *Adventures In Faith.* Thousands of books, tapes, and videos are distributed around the world every year through Jerry Savelle Ministries International.

**To order related material or sign up for our Correspondence School call, write or visit our website for further information.**

**Jerry Savelle Ministries International**
**P.O. Box 748**
**Crowley, TX 76036**
**817/297-3155**
**www.jsmi.org**

## Other Messages in our Freedom Series:

Free at Last from Oppression

Free at Last from Old Habits

Free at Last from Financial Lack

Free at Last from Repeated Distractions

Free at Last from Insecurity

Free at Last from Worry and Fear

Free at Last from Negative Thinking

## Other Books By Jerry Savelle

Free at Last from Old Habits

Thoughts - The Battle Between Your Ears

Expect the Extraordinary

In the Footsteps of a Prophet

The Last Frontier

Take Charge of Your Financial Destiny

From Devastation to Restoration

Walking in Divine Favor

Turning Your Adversity into Victory

Honoring Your Heritage of Faith

Don't Let Go of Your Dreams

Faith Building Daily Devotionals

The Force of Joy

If Satan Can't Steal Your Joy,
He Can't Keep Your Goods

A Right Mental Attitude

The Nature of Faith

Sharing Jesus Effectively

How to Overcome Financial Famine

## For those who don't know Jesus, would you like to know Him?

If you were to die today, where would you spend eternity? If you have accepted Jesus Christ as your personal Lord and Savior, you can be assured that when you die, you will go directly into the presence of God in Heaven. If you have not accepted Jesus as your personal Lord and Savior, is there any reason why you can't make Jesus the Lord of your life right now? Please pray this prayer out loud, and as you do, pray with a sincere and trusting heart, and you will be born again.

*Dear God in Heaven,*

*I come to You in the Name of Jesus to receive salvation and eternal life. I believe that Jesus is Your Son. I believe that He died on the cross for my sins, and that You raised Him from the dead. I receive Jesus now into my heart and make Him the Lord of my life. Jesus, come into my heart. I welcome You as my Lord and Savior. Father, I believe Your Word that says I am now saved. I confess with my mouth that I am saved and born again. I am now a child of God.*